WHAT NEAT FEET!

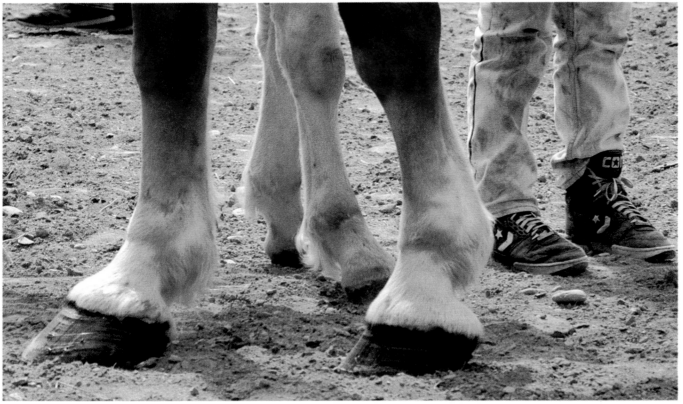

HANA MACHOTKA

Morrow Junior Books
New York

for Stoner

The text type is 20 pt. Avant Garde Gothic Book.

1 2 3 4 5 6 7 8 9 10
Library of Congress Cataloging-in-Publication Data
Machotka, Hana.
  What neat feet! / Hana Machotka.
    p. cm.
    Summary: Describes the foot of a swan, seal, rabbit, goat,
cat, camel, and elephant, and explains how the distinctive
design of each helps the animal survive in its environment.
    ISBN 0-688-09474-0.—ISBN 0-688-09475-9 (lib. bdg.)
    1. Foot—Juvenile literature.   [1. Foot.]   I. Title.
QL950.7.M29 1991
596'.049—dc20   90-40886   CIP   AC

Acknowledgments

Many of my photographs were taken at the Catskill Game Farm, Palenville, New York, and at the Bronx Zoo in New York City.

I express my special thanks to Susan Harris and Cindy Crosby of Pendleton Horse Farm, North Salem, New York, for their generous help with their horses; Dennis York and Darlene Commerford of the Commerford Petting Zoo in Goshen, Connecticut, for their time and patience with their elephant, Karen; and Vincent Vigilante for helping me with his rabbit.

As always, thanks to my editor, Andrea Curley, and to art director Ellen Friedman for their excellent input.

Feet are a very special part of the body. They are used to stand and to move on in the world. Feet can run, leap, bound, hop, walk, amble, or swim. Some feet can move over sand, snow, rocks, soil, or mud—even through the air or water.

In the animal kingdom, feet come in a great variety of shapes and forms. They can be hard or soft. They can be shaped like fins, flippers, paws, or hooves. But each foot is designed for that animal's particular needs and environment. The horse's hoof, for example, is very hard. Can you guess how it helps the horse live in its natural environment? As you look at the feet in this book, see if you can figure out how each one helps the animal live in its world.

This foot looks like a paddle and belongs to a...

SWAN

This webbed foot is formed by three long toes joined by a flap of skin. When the swan is on land, its foot can walk easily over a soft riverbank without getting stuck in the mud. In the water, it is a powerful propeller that enables the swan to move away from its enemies or toward food quickly.

When the swan is in flight, its feet fold up like an umbrella. With its feet out of the way, the swan can fly easily. When it wants to land on the water, its feet come down, open up, and slide over the water like a pair of water skis.

A foot shaped like a fin belongs on a...

SEAL

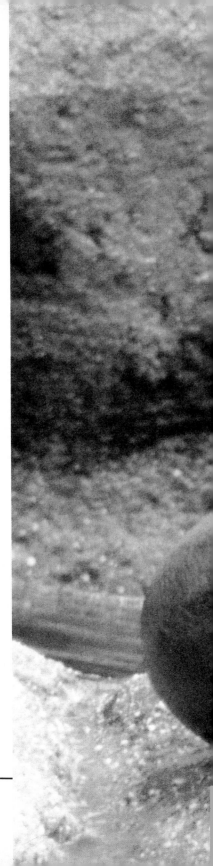

A seal's flipper is made up of five long fingers, or digits, covered by muscles and skin. Each digit ends in a nail, which is good for scratching an itch. The big front flippers are designed to steer, balance, and stop the seal as it glides through the water. As the seal's powerful muscles move it through the water, the smaller back flippers help to steer the seal.

When the seal wants to get up on some rocks to rest and dry off, it uses its front flippers to help hoist itself up out of the water. Once on land, the front and hind flippers move the seal's large body in an awkward, slithering motion.

These long, fuzzy feet belong to a...

RABBIT

With one big thrust, the muscles of these powerful feet can hurl a rabbit instantly away from danger. As the rabbit comes down again to the ground, its large feet with their soft pads act like shock absorbers to soften the landing. Sharp claws on the toes dig into the ground, giving the rabbit better balance and spring. In this way, the rabbit will bound along until it reaches the safety of its den.

A domestic rabbit may follow a person around like a puppy and can be walked on a leash. But watch out for those feet. If the rabbit is frightened, it may use its feet to knock the wind out of you!

This split hoof belongs to a ...

_____

GOAT

The two hard toes of a goat's hoof can spread around a rock and hold it tightly. The hard outside of the hoof acts to protect it from rocks. The soft, leathery middle of the hoof helps keep the goat from slipping. The two smaller toes above each hoof, called *dewclaws*, act as additional rock grippers.

These special feet make goats expert climbers. This is why they can live on the highest, steepest mountains, where few predators dare to go. Here goats can leap fearlessly from rock to rock.

A soft, padded foot that walks quietly belongs to a...

CAT

The domestic cat is descended from African wildcats and still possesses the build and nature of a hunter. It stalks its prey on silent, padded feet, then springs with its powerful hind feet. It grabs the prey with its forepaws, holding it with razor-sharp claws. The cat keeps its front claws ready for attack by sharpening them on trees or scratching posts. It keeps them from wearing down by pulling the nails up into the paw as it walks. The hind claws stick out like a dog's and get worn down.

A cat's pads are very sensitive. Did you ever see a cat paw an object as it tries to decide what it is?

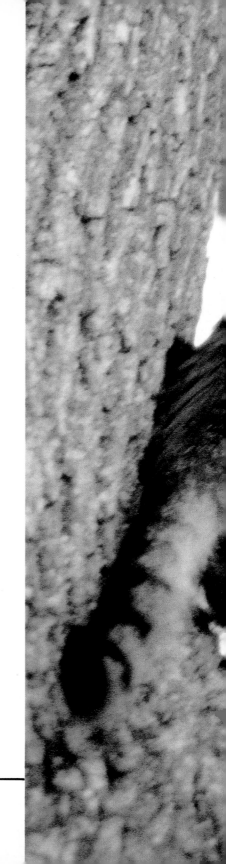

Leathery feet that walk on sand or snow belong to a...

CAMEL

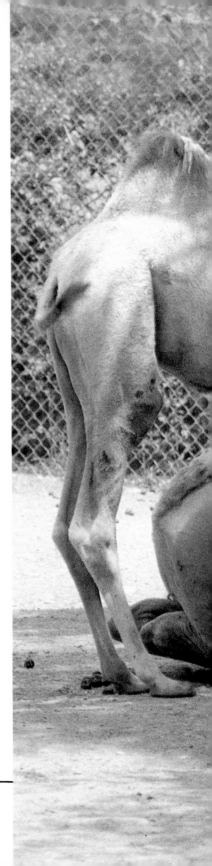

These two-toed feet are as large as dinner plates. As the camel walks, its toes spread apart without sinking into the sand.

A one-humped camel is called a *dromedary*. It is used for carrying people across the desert and even for racing. The two-humped camel is called a *Bactrian camel*. It has a strong build and can carry very heavy loads across high mountains. In the snow, its large feet spread out to work like snowshoes.

Camels are stubborn and sometimes pretend not to hear their owner's commands. They show their displeasure by grunting, groaning, or making faces.

A foot that looks like a tree trunk belongs to an...

ELEPHANT

This flat, round foot is like a cushion. It expands under the weight of the elephant and then gets smaller again when the elephant lifts its foot. This design helps keep the foot from getting stuck in the mud when the elephant goes down to a water hole for a drink or a bath.

Huge, round feet and legs provide a good support for such an enormous animal that eats hundreds of pounds of plants in a day. But this foot is not designed for speed. Although you might have to run to keep up with an elephant that's in a hurry, the fastest the elephant can move is at a quick walk.

We have seen that feet can do many jobs that help an animal live in its environment. Did you figure out what a horse's hooves can do? They are built to run swiftly over hard ground so the horse can escape its enemies. They can scratch an itch, fight, and dig up grass under the snow.

Now look at the swan's foot. Why is it different from a sparrow's? Why are your feet fleshy? What can they do?

Feet are special helpers that connect us to the earth while allowing us to live the way we do.